How The Power Of Habit Can Make You Thin
Mark Meakings

See Willy®

Published by: Gotham New Media,
PO Box 23,
Bexhill On Sea,
East Sussex,
TN39 4ZU
UK

Email info@seewilly.com
Web: www.seewilly.com

ISBN NO: 978-0-9559521-5-9

Illustrations by MAYANK A

Dedication

To: Professor Prokar Dasgupta and
Doctor Peter Amoroso

And the team at the
Prostate Cancer Centre, London.

For their dedication, talent, care
and wicked sense of humour.

Table of Contents

Disclaimer

This book reflects the authors' experiences and is provided for entertainment purposes and general reference only. It is not intended to be a substitute for medical or psychological advice or counselling. Therefore, you should consult a doctor and/or mental health professional regarding your individual physical and mental health needs before undertaking this diet assistance program or any diet, exercise, or fitness program. Results on this diet assistance program may vary. Neither the author nor publisher promises it will provide specific results from use of any content of this book.

FAQ's - DOUBTERS START HERE

Is losing weight, getting slim and feeling great for life really for you? Chances are yes and if so, here are some of the most common doubts and fears people experience before starting out:

Do I need 'will power' to succeed?
Nope. Will power and diets don't mix for long. The will power generally crumbles and you end up feeling lousy. You are going to use the power of auto-pilot habits that don't require will power, just being awake!

Can I get some quick results?
Yes, whilst rapid weight loss is not the idea here, you'll find you can start shedding pounds as soon as you begin taking control of your habits.

Is this just another 'diet' book?
No, I've seen too many fail. You won't find a single recipe, diet menu or calorie counter here.

What's different about this?
It uses the same techniques I created to stop myself smoking 40 a day for 15 years in an instant to achieve a life-changing 'shift' that few people experience that generally cannot be explained.

Can women use this book?
Yes, Although I wrote this for men who like me, don't 'do' diets, go to the gym, or buy women's weight loss magazines, the simple habit building methods I use apply to women as well. In fact, this is a complete system designed for 2 partners to work together on. Just select the habits you each feel comfortable with. If you have a partner doing this with you it will double your success rate! So instead of being nagged by your other half to follow her fad diet regime that never works, you have your own system for her to use with you.

Introduction

MY STORY AND WHY YOU NEED THIS BOOK

"Motivation is what gets you going. Habit is what keeps you going"
-Jim Rohn

Ladies and Gentlemen!

Welcome! Yes this is aimed at both of you even though only one of you has a willy!

This book is the culmination of 4 years of development work that contains a new system of slimming down and losing weight based on the power of habit.

It involves changes and if you are like me and many people I know, you may not find making change that comfortable. Maybe you're thinking like I used to i.e. "I crave it and can imagine just how good it would feel to be slim and healthier again, but I'm busy. And, quite frankly, I can't be bothered unless it's going to be easy!

So while doing this alone can definitely work for you (it did for me), having a partner buying into it and even doing it as well can magnify results.

Ladies, as well as getting a new slimmer partner, this is a great opportunity for you as well. If you've been thinking about slimming down, read and try this before you start your next diet.

This book is a powerful tool to help your partner slim down and get healthier and you can play a big part in helping him. Don't worry, it won't take much of your time, all you need do is read this book and then help support him in the Power Habit stage. The rest he can do on his own. Or if you want to follow the programme, you can help and support each other.

So, if you, or someone you love, wants to become the slimmer and fitter person they know they can be, start today by following the steps in this book.

Here's me when I started this book.

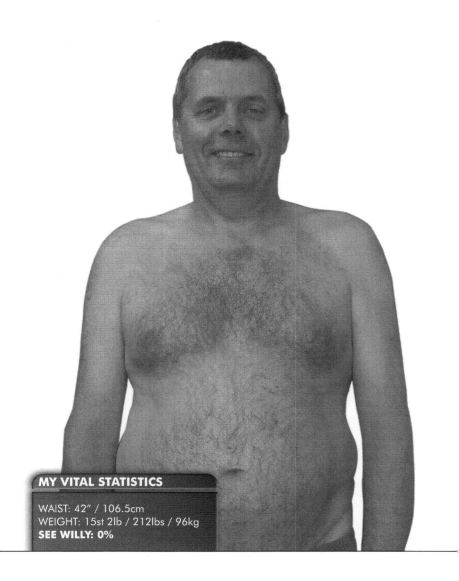

MY VITAL STATISTICS

WAIST: 42" / 106.5cm
WEIGHT: 15st 2lb / 212lbs / 96kg
SEE WILLY: 0%

Here's me when I finished

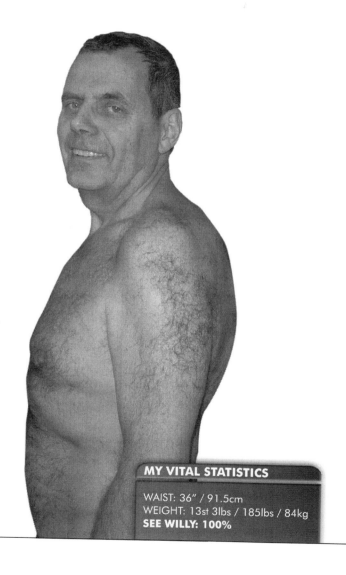

MY VITAL STATISTICS

WAIST: 36" / 91.5cm
WEIGHT: 13st 3lbs / 185lbs / 84kg
SEE WILLY: 100%

Eat All You Want And Never Gain Weight!

A REVOLUTION IN THE WEIGHT LOSS INDUSTRY

THROAT BAG

Introducing!

Eat A Ton **AND** Lose Weight
With Mark Meakings'
patented **THROAT BAG**

My patented system of inserting an opening hatch in the back of your neck that holds a bin liner finally cracks the weight problem!

Now you can enjoy every mouthful of anything as it goes straight out the back into the bin without putting an ounce of weight on!

Hmmm - I used to fantasize about this new invention of mine. Wouldn't it be great. But get real, it isn't going to happen any time soon!

It's about as daft as many of the other diet myths you read about. You see the diet industry is simply massive. It's based on the story that it's harder to get weight off than put it on. And that most people want to lose weight at some point in their lives without too much effort. That's why millions are invested in slimming pills.

So included in the many magic diets are pills that just lose water, foods that supposedly cause weight loss, exercise that on it's own won't make any difference except to your fitness levels, low fat diets that can cause you vitamin deficiencies, high fat diets that will clog up your arteries and many, many more.

The best way to lose weight and slim down is much simpler than you know.

I have created a new way of eating and living based on my techniques to build new habits on demand, without me even thinking about them. I have created these simply, easily and comfortably using my powerful techniques. It doesn't involve complicated dieting, calorie counts, gym workouts or anything else that would almost certainly never interest or motivate me or any of the people I know.

Not too terribly long ago, I felt like a miserable, bloated wreck. I felt sorry and disgusted for myself, and this had gone on for some time. I'd put on a whopping 28 pounds (or 2 stones from where I come from) in weight. I was "clinically obese" and miserable. But I didn't seem to be able to do anything about it. My clothes didn't fit. I was unable to sleep properly. My thinking was clouded. I was tired, and to complicate matters, my health began to fail.

I started to think just how often this was affecting my attitude and thoughts. From the moment I got up and showered, all through the day as I grappled with my tight clothes, as I looked enviously at others, as I hated myself for eating the massive meals in front of me. On and off all through the day!

I was feeling hopeless and helpless and just couldn't imagine I would ever be slim again.

It got so bad, I developed not one, but two, hernias. I also suffered from rather embarrassing bowel problems and ended up having to undergo scans because I was worried something "bad" was happening down there.

Oh, yes! To cap it all off, I had tremendous wind and suffered from those horrific and dreaded "skid" stools. You know what I'm talking about right!

For reasons beyond my ability to fathom now, all of this was happening while I continued to stuff my face at every turn. I ate two bowls of cereal instead of one when I didn't skip a "real" breakfast in favour of junk food. I just loved to late-night binge. I couldn't seem to make it through a day without multiple cappuccinos, cakes and other snacks. I was drinking a bottle of wine every couple of days and slurping far too much Guinness.

These actions had become habit - and these habits really were controlling my life.

They were my masters. I was their slave.

Habits are a force for good or bad. It doesn't really matter which side of the coin they fall on, they are the norm that we operate under. We just don't question them.

You see habits work subconsciously and have a wonderful way of making us feel comfortable with them, even if they are destroying our life. Changing habits is an uncomfortable business and usually doomed to failure. Unless you get inside them and use simple techniques to defeat and replace them.

Don't ask me why I did it, but I chose to put up with these habits and learn to cope with what seemed "normal" to me.

Fortunately, before things managed to get much worse, a bolt of lightning struck me while I was in one of the most unlikely places of all. Not perhaps in the fragrant clear air on a hill top, but in the hairy stench of a toilet in a motorway service station on the M25! (for everyone else who doesn't know, this is a ring freeway that circles around London.)

I'd driven to a meeting and, as usual, skipped breakfast, overdosed on coffee and cakes on the way there and in the meeting. Now, driving home, I was desperate for a pee (it's harder to cork it when you are overweight).

So I pulled up almost falling backwards out of the car in my haste to point the key fob at it whilst on the run to not pee my pants and ended up going into the toilets with three other men who were together.

To cap it all off, all three wore thin T-shirts, were slim and made me feel self-conscious about my huge belly.

So, as you do, we all unzipped almost at the same time. Hands down to willy and the welcome warm relief of disgorging my distended bladder started to wash over me. Bliss!

But you know how it is; it was a long pee. In fact I never thought it would end. We all feel less than comfortable at these urinals. I don't see why we can't be more like the girls and have our own private space.

These guys were friends and carried on talking across me. With one to my left and two to my right and trying not to feel embarrassed at my comparative huge size (my belly!), I tried my best to hold it in so I could at least feel normal. But I'd forgotten that I'd gone past the point where anything but a sprung corset could keep it in, so I gave up and relaxed and let it all fold out neatly. God, the embarrassment!

I'm told when women go for a smear, they pretend to be somewhere else to blot out the experience. I thought I'd try it. So I decided to focus on the facing wall and engross myself in the sales poster (why we can't even pee without being sold to I don't know!).

Well, as it happened, I wasn't in the market for the strawberry flavoured condoms being sold to me on the poster. I started to glance left and right, but if you've ever been in this situation, you know to quickly look away. Otherwise someone may think you have penis envy or are a pervert!

There was only one way to go. Look down...

... that was the exact moment that changed my life!

As soon as my eyes wandered down to avoid looking like a perv, I realised there was a terrible problem.

"Bloody hell, WHERE'S MY WILLY!" I shouted to myself in my mind. "I can't even see my willy! All I can see is a mountain hanging down from my tits!"

And, oh God, my tits looked like they needed support as well!

I started to get very hot. Judging from the evidence on either side of me, I quickly determined that my willy was about par for the course as far as size was concerned. (At least I believe it was. After all, I could no longer see it!)

I also watched one of the guys look down at his own willy (he was a bit strange looking!). But I could clearly see that he could see his willy without the aid of a stomach harness, bending over or with the aid of mirrors!

But all I could see was my belly. It was massive, looking forever like a heaving mass of pastry rolling down to obscure my willy from me! Could this really be me?! Had I really let myself go this far?!

In that moment I finally woke up!

I instantly became determined to drive all the way to that urinal again, have a pee and see my willy!

I'd been so busy with the rest of my life, building my businesses and making a name for myself, that I nearly forgot who I am and what I do. I teach people computer, Internet and life-changing skills for a living and I had the knowledge, skills and know-how to make this goal a rather easy one for myself. After all, if I could help others attain their goals, surely I could help myself be able to see my willy once more!

Once the clouds cleared from my habit-addled brain, I remembered I had developed strategies that enabled me to stop smoking in an instant after 15 years of heavy smoking. I did this with no patches, zero effort or even side effects. That was 28 years ago and I haven't craved a cigarette once since.

At the time I gave up smoking, I was a cabin crew member for British Airways working on Concorde. I was very proud to be working on this angel of an aircraft and we were the elite of cabin crew. We didn't work hard (the max flight time was 3.5 hours and then we'd get a couple of nights in a 5 star hotel) but we did drink hard and smoke hard. We partied and had a fun life.

But my smoking was getting out of hand and I was having chest problems. I would light up sometimes before getting out of bed, I'd smoke 30 to 40 a day. As soon as Concorde's wheels left the deck, I would be in one of the toilets having a cigarette (something happily you can't do nowadays on any aircraft). I had access to cheap cigarettes, which simply fuelled the habit and made it much easier for me to feed it. I was a heavy smoker, plain and simple.

My success with kicking the cigarette habit was based on an early version of my habit system that I discovered by accident. I'd spent 2 years desperately trying to give up with no success. Here's a typical event that would leave me feeling helpless and depressed about my smoking.

I had worked a flight from Bahrain to London and arrived home with a new carton of 200 cigarettes. It was winter and I sat down in front of our small open fire with this carton in my hand. I worked up every ounce of will power I could muster. I told myself all the great things that would happen if I didn't smoke them. I'd feel great, I'd breathe more easily, my clothes wouldn't smell and on and on.

I took a deep breath and threw the carton on the fire. It was late at night so I knew there was nowhere to go to get some more (local shops closed in the evenings then). I sat there feeling wonderful.

At 2 a.m. I was desperately searching the house for a cigarette. There were none. I was reduced to finding a cigarette butt of an old one in the trash.

Did I feel like a drug addict? You bet! And I felt so bad at the same time.

My habit master was back in control of my life. This type of event was repeated for 2 years!

Finally, I started to look more closely at the true power of 'habit' and I developed some simple techniques that enabled me on a memorable fine summers day in a pub to simply say, "no thanks, I don't smoke" to my friend who was offering.

I achieved a paradigm "shift" in my consciousness in an instant.

I did this just as easily as if someone had flicked a mental smoking switch from on to off. Just like a "lights on", "lights off" switch.

In all these years I never stopped marvelling at how easy this finally was and how lucky I was to escape this destructive habit. I managed to walk away from it using techniques I'll show you here to loose your flab and see your willy.

So, the question was clear. Why on earth wasn't I using my own techniques to lose my belly? The answer was plain. It was because I was living on autopilot, being controlled by powerful destructive bad habits. I was sleep walking along and it took my meeting at the urinals to wake me up. To remind me I already had the solution, but these habits were so powerful, they were blinding me to them.

So when you see the experience I have, you will also see the awe inspiring power "habit" had over me. I was living a miserable life completely on automatic and in full acceptance of it being "normal."

As I was living my own personal nightmare, I was teaching others how to improve their lives. And, all the while I had been asleep to helping myself.

My time had come and yours has too! Sit back, loosen your belt, let it all hang out and learn to use my techniques to help you see willy.

If I could do it, you can too! And, trust me, realizing this goal is not difficult at all if you rely on the power of habits to make it so.

The payoff? Well, just imagine being able to see your willy again! Imagine your wife or partner's reaction to the new, improved you! Picture being able to go to the loo without wanting to hide your face or run in embarrassment!

I've been back to that motorway service station. I've seen the promised land. The good news is you can have it too!

Chapter One

Habit Is Stronger Than Reason

I'm a bloke, you're a bloke (probably). I think we'd agree, we don't do "diets" or belong to weight loss clubs. Only one of my friends uses a gym. If you are like me, you don't have the time and especially the inclination to read massive diet books that tell us what we already probably know, but quickly get bored with.

Oh pleeeaaasseee.......! When you talk to me about diets, my eyes start to glaze over and I head off for a beer or a glass of wine. Carrot sticks are not my friends!

"Just remind me of the basics. If I happen to have been feeling smug, this will remind me how awful my situation is. Then, in words of two syllables or less, give me the cure! And I only want to know if it'll work all my life. I was 6 when I had my last yo-yo. I quickly got bored with it and don't have time to play with another one. I need a toy, or a plan, that will bloody well last!"

If this rings your bell, this book is for you. I can help you lose your belly and reintroduce you to your willy!

No, I'm not going to bore you at length with what you already know about the health risks of being overweight. I can't say they were uppermost in my mind at the urinal. But, just to add to your motivational juices, here's a summary to remind yourself there are some pretty awesome benefits to be had.

Obesity caused by overeating is the biggest cause of death in the Western world.   At least one in three of us needs to lose weight. It's not just not being able to wear the clothes we want, it creates diseases like asthma, diabetes, high blood pressure and arthritis. Simply put, obesity kills people; lots of people!

If you are overweight, there are a host of other problems you are likely to be at greater risk from. Hernias, piles, eczema are just a few. In many cases, heart disease is brought on by being overweight. If you Google some of these you'll see that you are more at risk of a heart attack and stroke, going blind or losing limbs with diabetes, or even more at risk if you have an operation under general anaesthetic.

The long and the short, or the fat and the thin of it is that losing weight will help your body in many ways. You will feel less strain on your back, your knees, your hips and even your feet. You will feel better about yourself. You will make a real, noticeable and tangible difference in your life.

Okay, that's the end of the scary stuff. Well, no, not all of it anyway. Putting yourself at these odds of becoming ill, or debilitated, or dying isn't just a personal hazard. Our friends and close family become badly affected in all sorts of ways and it can have a devastating effect on them, too.

But, if you are like me, the reason that will motivate you is the emotional and highly personal one. I simply want to be in control of myself and feel great for being so.
I WANTED TO SEE MY WILLY again, get in the suit, feel great, feel foxy, etc.

Oh, and by the way, it's also a great feeling to not have all those risks, as well. Seeing willy, however, is the motivation that works. Go with what strikes your fancy.

The truth is we make ourselves fat and we can make ourselves unfat. Babies are not obese. We overeat for psychological and physical reasons. It's only when we decide to take control, make the right choices and stop making excuses our lives will change.

People over eat and eat bad food for many reasons. Often when they are feeling depressed, anxious, sad, under stress or even when they are deliriously happy. That fact is most of us don't really need much of a reason to over eat.

More often than not, though, over eating is nothing more than a collection of bad habits. After all, it's almost impossible to eat properly in today's hectic world. Or, is it?

Yes, this is exactly what I used to think before I started researching my own plan to ditch my belly, see my willy and start feeling great again. The solution is more powerful and yet more simple than you can imagine.

What worked for me was setting up my new habit programme to support me as I cleaned out my system, cut out bad carbohydrates and sugar and cut down on alcohol.

I gradually reduced the size of meals from the mountain on a plate to a reasonable size. I started eating the right food and filling up on protein and vegetables. Oh yes, I did even work on moving around a touch more. Nothing too complicated, mind you. But, impossible to maintain over time unless you have a seriously powerful ally working with you all day and every day.

How do you overcome with ease that feeling you wake up with every morning when you say "I'm going to be better today," but when it comes down to it you don't? You know the feeling: You're hungry and about to eat. You cave in and your good intentions go right out the window. Alas, tomorrow is another day.

This is the trap of believing that "mind over matter" will work. We foolishly believe our strength of will might prevail over our attraction to stuff ourselves full of rubbish. Unfortunately, it rarely does.

Can this trap be avoided? Can we actually overcome?

Absolutely! But, you see most people are not easily able to align their behaviour with their intentions.

When do vegetables and fruit cease to be those "annoying" things you should eat but don't really want to. How can you make them become as appealing as a burger or fizzy drink?

Use the most amazing and irresistible power to help you and you will never think or feel the same way about food again. You'll finally take control of your body and your life and enjoy all the benefits that go with it like:

Improved self-esteem - There is nothing quite like looking in the mirror and realising you no longer need a corset to look like a strapping bloke!

Better outlook on life - When you take control of your body and see your dreams materialise, your entire outlook on life will change. Rather than feel like a pawn in someone else's game, you'll believe in yourself and your ability to tackle anything.

Better health - Whilst losing weight and being able to see your willy once again won't guarantee you better health, it will sure help you increase your odds. (Refer back to those scary conditions I spoke about earlier. Your chances of developing these will go down!)

Being able to see your willy - And, herein lies the kicker. You will not only be able to reacquaint yourself with your willy, you won't be embarrassed to take a pee in a public toilet! You will, in short, be that lean, mean fighting machine you (and perhaps your significant other) have dreamed of.

So, what is this magical power?

It's time to get REWIRED using the power of HABIT!

Chapter Two

Who You Are Today Is Governed By Your Habits

When we look at eating habits, some would say "I can't help myself, it's my nature to be fat" Wrong! Our eating habits create part of our nature. What we repeatedly do becomes habit and habits form our nature, which in turn forms the way we eat and live.

"We first make our habits, and then our habits make us."

With so much at stake, having good or having bad habits leads to success or failure, happiness or misery in so many aspects of life.

Our habits are either the best of servants or the worst of masters.

So why not just change habits to suit us? So many people try and fail without understanding how habits are formed and how to use them as servants instead of masters.

It's not willpower that is needed, just understanding and simple habit changing techniques.

If you think that breaking old habits and forming new ones can't change your life, think again! I'm living, breathing and willy-seeing proof that this is so. Psychologists even wax poetic about the powers of habit.

Functional psychologists William James and John Dewey dedicated a great deal of their professional lives studying the power of habit. In his "Principles of Psychology," James pointed to habit as the fundamental building block found in human behavior.

Habits are not formed overnight. They are cultivated over time. (They are not like fine wine in many cases. Some habits just don't get better! Overeating, smoking and drinking too much, for example, are habits none of us should cultivate!)

Now, back to those habits and how they form. When a person repeats an action over and over again, it eventually becomes an ingrained habit. Scientific research has shown that the brain's neurons actually create a pathway that enables them to move from a habit's trigger point, such as drinking a cup of coffee, to performing the habit. Let's say smoking in this case.

How long it takes the brain to develop pathways that support habits depends on the complexity of the action involved. Very basic, simple habits can be hammered into the brain in no time at all. Basic habits that require little thought, for example, can be worked into a person's behavior patterns in as little as 28 days if they are repeated again and again.

If you doubt the power of habits in life - yours or anyone else's - just take a look at yourself or others. Habits are a part of who you are. They are a part of your friends, family and the people you meet on the street.

Look around you at others and you will quickly see that habit is a force to be reckoned with. Some common habits aren't necessarily bad, but they are prevalent and serve as good examples as to the power of this magic and include:

Following crowds - Somewhere along the way, humans must have picked up a pack mentality gene! Just look at what people in airports do. They get off the plane and follow each other in a tight, close-knit pack. Only a few will break free from the crowd.

Forgetting keys - Some people always, always, always leave their keys in the house in the morning. The action is so ingrained, it's second nature to go back inside and get them. On the flipside, some hang their keys up the second they walk in the door. They do this so often, they don't even think about the action. It is automatic!

Ordering the same foods in restaurants - When you eat out at a favourite restaurant, do you always order the same fare? Chances are you do! You're not alone. This is a habit that many of us form over time. Some of us even have our own favourite dishes that we order at different eateries. Don't believe this is habit? Consider your reaction if that restaurant didn't have what you wanted on the menu for whatever reason. Would you be disappointed, perhaps even lost? You bet you would! That's called habit.

Always taking the same locker at the gym or seat in the boardroom - Do you have a propensity to go to the same places over and over again? A lot of people do. That's called habit.

The examples of habits can go on and on and on. They are strong. They are powerful. They are uncomfortable to break. So, why not just replace them with new ones? It feels a whole lot better and it can have a powerful effect on your life.

The simple truth of the matter is that some habits are good. Some habits can protect us and even shield our sanity in this crazy world. Others, sadly, are just plain bad and can even kill us.

Looking at habits that surround your eating and exercise behaviors are just two small areas in the overall picture that makes you who you are. If you change these habits - replace the bad with the good - you will change your life!

So maybe you are thinking your current eating and exercise (or lack of) habits are powerful because you get (temporary) enjoyment from them. Maybe you love burgers and chips.   So how can new ones that sound boring compete with these?

Imagine this. Right now when you gorge on burger and fries and a few pints of beer you'll probably be feeling fine and enjoying yourself. But, you'll be less than happy with the consequences of this each and every day, all day. Fat, bloated, ashamed, envious of others are just a few of the associated feelings.

Now imagine the new habits in place.

You won't be craving fries. Once you get out of the habit of certain foods, they actually taste different. As a single example fried chips lose taste and you can really go off them. It's the same for other junk food. Your taste buds will start to crave good natural food instead. You'll also find being stuffed full becomes a horrible feeling. If you suffer indigestion or have a hiatus hernia, the problem will often completely disappear. You feel and look great and your confidence will be very high.

So can you now see, your new habits are actually a lot more positive and healthy than your old ones.

Habits are so powerful you can't change them on a whim. They have cemented themselves into your being over time and will not let go without a fight. So, what you need to do is to consciously develop new habits that gradually replace the old. In simple terms, if you do something for 28 days or thereabouts it tends to become a habit.

Brain researchers have shown that when we consciously develop new habits we create parallel synaptic paths and even entirely new brain cells that can jump over our train of thought onto new tracks. We can direct our own change by consciously developing new habits. The more we try, the more we step outside our comfort zone. These new habits can bypass old ones.

Chapter Three

Starting Out And Your Thinking Habits

I am asking you to put aside everything you may have been told about weight loss, to open your mind to the simple and obvious solutions I have created for you here. To use your own common sense and intuition to question and then realize that there are good reasons diets fail and there are powerful, simple ways to creating a new you. A new you that quickly finds your own natural, comfortable and healthy weight. That maintains this weight without thought or effort, but only with pleasure.

The information given here is different in that it represents a new understanding in the field of weight loss. It doesn't build on anything before it. It will lift a veil for you and reveal why you do what you do and what you can do about it that actually works - for life!

This will happen with a change to your thinking habits, re-enforced by some simple work on your day-to-day physical habits.

So please approach this with an open and inquisitive mind. Don't be put off if any of the solutions appear simplistic. If you make a commitment and take a little time to understand your thinking habits around weight loss and make a few corrections, you will make that life-changing reverse 'shift' easier.

I know this sounds like a pipe dream, but if you are really serious about changing your life, then all I ask you to do is be open to read and re-read this book in its entirety before you draw your conclusions.

Commitment

Without commitment success in weight loss management is going to be difficult.   When you make the commitment you are saying to yourself "I can see myself today as slim and fit, I'm really excited this is on the way into my life! - there's absolutely no doubt about it, it's coming now!"

This is a more positive message than "I will eat less today" or "I will stick to my eating habits today".

Can you see why? Well the first commitment quickly becomes an emotional commitment. You get to 'feel' great about this when you make it. And when you feel great, you can't help but attract it into your life as you will see.

Commitment is a powerful tool that takes away any half-hearted approach. Make the commitment now and make it a habit to renew your commitment every day. Do this by making an entry in a diary, sending your self repeat email commitments, putting up a sticky at your bedside to see every morning as you get up (before you start eating).

Your Thinking Habits Determine How You Feel and, How You Feel Can Make Or Break Your Weight Loss Success

OK, remember the 'open mind'? If you are a habitual negative thinker this is where you may need it. Stick with me and use your intuition.

Everything begins with a thought and ends with positive or negative attraction.

Here's the simple story.

1 You have a thought.

2 You have an associated feeling and emotional response.

3 You vibrate in low or high frequencies depending on the feeling.

4 You attract into your life the same vibrations given off by other people on the same frequency.

"Are you nuts!?"

Stick with me, you experience this every day, you just haven't woken up to it. It's the law of the universe. Some call it the "law of attraction" and used wisely it will guarantee your life long success in managing your weight and fitness.

We are all living magnets and we attract into our lives whatever we are 'vibrating'. We are all made up of atoms and cells like every other 'thing' in the universe. We all vibrate.

Imagine a room full of tuning forks of different sizes so when you ring each one, it has a different frequency. The room is silent and you walk in carrying a single tuning fork. You ring it. Any tuning fork on the same frequency will also ring whilst the others remain silent.

Make sense? Of course it does.

Now put this into real life. You are in a room full of people. Someone walks in who "really lights up the place". Everything about them gives off high frequency, positive vibrations. Guess what? Only those people operating on a similar frequency will be attracted to that person to make contact. Others operating on a lower, more negative frequency will not be attracted into the persons life. Both of these people would feel very uncomfortable with each other.

You know this makes sense, it's been happening all your life. You see it everywhere everyday.

So how can this help you slim down and maintain a healthy weight? Stick we me.

Operating on a higher positive frequency naturally attracts other positive people, events and even so called 'co-incidences" into your life - automatically. You don't need to do anything else! Think about how this applies to some of the people you know. What frequencies do you think they operate on and what type of people and events do they seem to 'automatically' attract into their lives?

So, flip back to the start - ALL of this originates from your original thinking.

Change your thinking - change your life!

Change your thinking habits around weight loss and some of your eating habits and you are guaranteed life-long success.

You always get what you think about. Think negatively and get more of the same. Think positively and get more of the same.

Think "I don't want to be fat anymore" and guess what you get? More fat.

Think "I'm really excited about being slim" and guess what you get? Slim!

Here's an example of how this universal law works.

Here's how it works in reality. I have been feeling very 'up' about my new computer learning books. I had been asked to appear on QVC TV with them and had a great response from people. There really wasn't much for me to be doing (I like to work a 6 hour work week so I can spend my time enjoying life with my other interests) and I got to think about my retail distributors. They are very positive people and feel 'good' to be around. I always come away from seeing them 'feeling' happy and positive.

I am 'attracted' to them. We 'vibrate' on the same frequencies. It's 'inevitable' we will want to spend time together.

There was no specific reason for me to drive 150 miles to share coffee with them, but nevertheless, I 'felt' motivated to do so.

On arrival I was made very welcome and we talked about

my new books. It turns out they could help with marketing these in ways I never imagined and I was very grateful.

Just as I was leaving I experienced a 'co-incidence' that could have far reaching effects for me.   There was a picture of a ship on the wall of the hotel lounge. It 'reminded' me that I had my training products used on cruise ships many years ago and prompted me to mention this in passing.

It turns out the distributor knew someone who was specifically working with cruise ships on new products for their on board computer learning centres and he gave me his name.

This resulted in a meeting with this person and as a result my products may once again be available 'at sea' and we may be taking a cruise or two to go with them.

AND I play drums with a band and have joked for a year about playing a gig on a cruise ship. I have thought about it and imagined it and even experienced how it would feel many times. Guess what? This person will put me directly in touch with the person who books the entertainers.

I find I experience positive "co-incidences" all the time. They open up new opportunities for me. Some come to nothing and some have literally changed the course of my life.

This all came about, this attraction to life changing opportunities and events simply because I was thinking positive thoughts, 'feeling' good and vibrating at a high level and as a result was motivated to 'move' to get together with people of a similar positive attraction.

It's not always easy, but making a habit to check your thoughts is probably the single most powerful way to change and improve your life. Feel good as a result of your thoughts. Thoughts lead to vibrations, vibrations lead to attractions (good or bad).

So the real power is thoughts.

Everything originates from thought. Thought creates feeling and emotion. This creates vibration. Whatever level you vibrate at, you will attract more of the same into your life. It's the law of universe.

Now, guess what. If I had spent my time thinking about how bad it felt to be fat, how embarrassed it made me feel, how it was going to rain all day, how everyone else's problems were getting me down - what do you think I would attract into my life?

Yes, certainly. More of the same! Day in, day out. More of the same.

I want you to focus on your thinking about weight loss. You may think your thoughts are 'automatic'. They are not. You were not wired with them from birth. You learned these over a long period of time. Here's the key.

Once you become aware of them as they happen, you have the power to change them and never look back. Like the physical habits you will acquire, these new thinking habits will become comfortable and then even exciting and certainly automatic.

Your personal tuning fork will begin to vibrate at a higher frequency - stand back as you will be amazed at your success with weight loss and surprised with all the high frequency life changing opportunities that start to appear in front of you.

So remember, your thoughts are not 'automatic' and that they originate from you. Master the technique of monitoring them and making simple conscious decisions with them. The result is truly life-changing.

Every moment of every day you are having thoughts. You create them subconsciously in most cases and most of the time they are negative. I can prove this for you now. Make a card and write on it "what am I thinking now" - examine it and see if it's positive or down.

Example - "Won't it ever stop raining!"

Now the thought didn't just appear on its own - you created it. And this is normally by your attitude.

Guess how that thought makes you feel? Yes, down. And now you are down you are vibrating at the bottom of the scale. Keep doing that all day and every day is a drag! Nothing new, exciting or positive is going to be attracted to you.

Don't feel bad, that's how most people operate every day of their lives. And it's why 'positive' change is so hard for them. They don't attract anything positive into their lives. You have to consciously work at it.

If you don't believe you need feelings to create happiness consider this.

Try this now. Just say "I feel happy" quickly. Doesn't work does it?

You can't apply logic or brute thinking force to get what you want.

You need to relax, let go negative thoughts and re-focus on positive ones.

Then the feeling comes. Then you are vibrating on a high frequency. Then you attract positive people, events and results AUTOMATICALLY into your life. Just sit back in the certain expectation they will appear. It's the law of the universe.

Ultimately just as you are what you eat, you also are what you think about.

So now let's just focus on your negative thoughts around your weight.

Don't worry this isn't going to get deeper here. All I want you to do is be aware of your negative thinking around your weight and have a simple plan to combat it and turn the power of thought to your advantage. To help you use and cement the powerful 'physical' habits in this book, to once and for all get lifelong control of your weight.

Let's just focus on just 2 places. Your bathroom mirror and your pocket. First your mirror.

Every time you look at yourself or catch a glance of yourself in a mirror you have a negative thought. Maybe it's 'God, I'm fat", "when will I ever be thin', "I'll never be strong enough to lose all this weight" etc.

Any and all similar thoughts lead to? Yes, you guessed it. You 'FEEL' bad.

And feeling bad means you vibrate on a low frequency, virtually guaranteeing you will just get more of the same!

Now these thoughts really are not 'automatic'. They don't just appear. You weren't born with them. YOU learned over a long time, you create them and from them your feelings flow and from them your power of attraction to positive life events and changes.

So what can you do to change your thinking and lose that weight?

Simple. Become aware of your thoughts around your body and weight, stop them and replace them with positive thoughts.

Sound too easy? Yep, it really is that simple, but like the rest of my habit building techniques in this book, you need to make it into a new habit.

Here's how one powerful situation will help you enormously.

Put a sign up on your bathroom mirror that reads, "what am I thinking now?"

So now as you stand in the buff out of the shower, you get a really good look at yourself.

You will become aware of the negative thoughts and feelings you usually have.

But this time stop and think a bit more. These negative thoughts will affect only you. When you leave the bathroom, no one else will know or care about them.

Just you. It's just you that's left 'feeling bad'. And you know what happens with bad feelings - yes, they just attract more of the same.

Keep thinking negatively about 'how fat you are' and guess what? Yep, you're smack on course for more of the same.

Perhaps now you're thinking, this is getting too 'touchy feely' for me. The next thing he's going to tell me is to 'visualize' myself thin looking in the mirror!

Well no actually. All I want you to do is to catch the negative thought. Ask yourself what will you feel if you decide to follow this chain of thought and then DECIDE not to. Yes, that's right, as soon as the thought appears, let it go. Don't focus on it.

The easiest way to replace the thought is to focus on the moment. On this moment right now. So for example, look out the window, have some simple 'grateful' thoughts for the trees, or birds or sky or anything happening in the here and now. Until the negative train of thought has gone.

Then just move on with your daily life.

If you find yourself starting to think negatively about your weight during the day, be sure to trap the thought, question what possible use it is and where it will lead you to in a chain of negative thoughts.

Downhill is the answer.

Have 2 thinking tactics in place to deal with it. Either works.

1   Let the thought drift away and think "I'm really excited about being slim - it's on its way into my life"

2   Let the thought drift away and focus on the moment instead. Look around you at anything and think about it. Preferably in gratitude. "I'm so lucky to be in this car out of the rain", "I'm so pleased I can touch type", "the sun is really beautiful". There is beauty and wonder in everything. Just think about it until the negative weight thought has finally disappeared. Then check yourself in a few minutes and compare how you are feeling to how you know you would have been feeling if you had followed your normal negative thoughts.

Keep an open mind and keep it up until it becomes habit to think positively and feel better about your weight. You will slip up, that's OK we all do.

Get to the stage where you are so aware of your negative thoughts about your weight you don't take them seriously any more. If they are negative, you are aware of it. You don't start to analyze the thought, you just say, "whoops another one" and send it on it's way while you focus on the moment or happier thoughts.

Getting rid of your negative thinking about your weight, frees you up to choose your selection of physical habits to acquire from this book and really apply yourself. You will loose the 'self defeatist' attitude that wrecks peoples' so called 'iron will' to lose weight and get fit.

Once you realize that your success lies in developing simple automatic thinking and doing habits, you'll wonder what all the fuss is about and be able to get on enjoying your life.

Life is not what makes you who you are - your thoughts and habits do.

Now you know how to create your own thinking habits to attract a positive healthy weight, you are ready to start un-locking the amazing power of physical habits.

Chapter Four

A Little Motivation

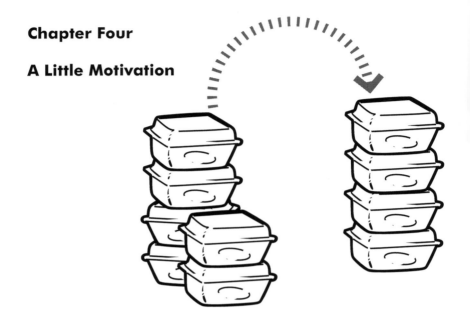

Once you begin to notice the weight dropping away and your clothes starting to fit, this may be all the motivation you need to continue with your habit-building programme. However, when you first start out you need some way to measure your success that creates an impact on your positive feelings and motivates you.

Sure you can pop on the scales every day. But after a while the numbers seem to lose their power. You even forget what progress you have been making on a weekly basis. You can't SEE the fat loss.

Until now!

Start now by collecting all your empty butter packs. Wash them out and keep them. It will take too long to collect enough of your own for our purposes, so ask family, friends and colleagues to help you. I did this and collected over 40 packs in no time.

Find a place in your house where you will have room to store 2 piles of them. Next look at the packs. They are normally 1/4 pound packs, but sometimes 1/2 pounds packs. See yourself as being slim again and do a quick estimate of how many pounds you intend to lose. Let's say for example it's 30 pounds. Using our butter packs to represent this means 30 times 4, 1/4 pound packs or 120 packs! That's far too many to collect quickly and you want to get going now.

So start with a 10-pound pile. Start by neatly stacking 10 times 4, 1/4 pound packs into a 40 stack.

Think about the butter that was in each of these packs. It's not a long way off imagining them full of fat!

So every day, before you eat breakfast note your weight. Then every time you see a loss of 1/2 a pound, move 2 of the empty butter packs to a new stack beside the first one. This is the stack that shows you 'physically' how much fat you are loosing.

Watching that stack grow is a fantastic feeling!

Spend a minute or two thinking about these and congratulating yourself on your progress.

Just imagine you started out carrying 120 packs of butter tied to your waist.

Now you start watching them disappear from your 'body' adding to your 'fat' stack. Eventually, they'll be gone!

So keep collecting the butter packs as you watch the first 40 move. You will be able to add to your body pack until you get to 120.

Just imagine seeing half of these disappear from your body. Look at the 'fat' stack and remind yourself you no longer have to find the energy to carry these around. They are no longer filling out your waist, your double chins, your fat thighs!

This idea came to me when I found myself binge eating a long time ago. All I had in the fridge was a pack of butter and some old fruit and vegetables. Sad, I know. I'd pretty much eaten everything else!

Since there wasn't anything else to crave over in the fridge, I started to think about the butter and the pack it was in. It looked so much like fat to me. I knew it was a 1/4 pound pack without even looking.

I know of no other better way to motivate me to build my own habits and I recommend it to you.

Chapter Five

Your Power Habit Plan

What follows is a series of new habits you can form to show you, first and foremost, the power of habits and how easy they are to develop. You will then find new habits that can impact your eating, drinking and exercise behaviors for the better.

Work through section 1 before you move on. Then take 2 habits from each of the Power Habit sections to build on. Habits take time to create and cement, so don't be in a rush, take your time to make sure you have created long lasting habits from each section before moving on to more Power Habits to work on.

Because you will be building these new habits gradually, you will find the process easy and comfortable and your odds of long-term success will be far greater. If you jump around sections to begin with firing off too many new habits, you will fail.

Next, don't be afraid to mutilate the book. Tear out the habits for reference; write over it, whatever works for you. I read a great deal and my respect is generally for the content, not for the physical book itself.

If you are reading this as an e-book, then you'll find readers resources at the website www.seewilly.com

OK, Habits 1 to 10 are preparation habits.

These are unrelated to weight, but are important as they are your grounding in habit forming and will give you confidence when you work with the really important ones.

Habits 11 to 20 are power habits designed to change your eating patterns.

Habits 21 to 24 are designed to change your drinking habits

Habits 24 to 34 are designed to get you moving more.

Habits 35 to 86 are optional supporting habits.

The 24 Power Habits of eating, drinking and exercise above, are few by design. I could have doubled these, but if you are like me, and have a short attention span, that would be overkill. So I have given you the minimum you need to see your willy.

There are many more great habits to help you from 35 to 86, but these are not essential. Wait until you have your main habits under your belt before you experiment with them.

Start with 1 to 10 to get used to consciously developing new habits on autopilot and to feel success. See their power before moving on to 11 onwards that will set you up for a new slim and fit life - for life!

Remember, when you build habits, you build automatic re-actions. It's the mind switch that takes over. To help yourself along the way, focus on a few habits at a time. Make them yours. Once you have, move on to a few more.

I use little tricks to help me make my goal habits my automatic reactions. Visualisation, post-it notes, mental movies and patience all work wonders.

It generally takes 28 days for significant habits to take hold. So, in that period, you will need to be sure to have constant reminders with you or in front of you at the appropriate time you need them.

Habits at work can be on screen, use the stickies program or Post-it notes as a reminder.

Others can be written out as a few words and placed wherever you need them. You can, for example, post your notes on the TV, fridge, front door, car dashboard etc.

For other situations, for example, new eating out habits and shopping habits you will need a card or a mental movie to refer to each time BEFORE you enter a restaurant or a grocery store.

Even tear out the left page of each HABIT and use it as your 28-day mentor! Don't worry about the book, it's just paper and can be recycled. If you are reading this as an e-book, then you'll find readers resources at the website www.seewilly.com

This book gives you the tools to change the way you live in a gradual and powerful way that will become your new preferred way of living. Use it to your advantage.

Chapter Six

Preparation Habits

Cut out the HABITS LIST from the back of the book or get them at the website www.seewilly.com or write them onto sticky Post-it notes.

Put the start date on each new habit as today and the end date as 28 days from now.

Place the habit sticky so that you cannot miss seeing it at the exact time you are about to perform the normal habit. Then perform the new habit. That's all for now.

Choose any 2 of the first 10 Preparation Habits that follow. It's very important you don't move beyond these until they are completed. So ideally your real weight loss will begin after the first 28 days. Be patient! It's taken you a long time to get the way you are. You need to experience the true power of habit before you apply it to changing your life.

Practice these on a daily basis and never miss a day. Don't move on until you have developed the new habits and they feel completely comfortable and automatic. You don't have to succeed in all of them, but aim for at least 2 successes.

Habit 1

Stop Watching TV News!

DOWN

STRIKE

DJHEH -12.21   DHYEI -0.04 FJEF -2.53 GHIJR -344 HJKF 423

Severely restrict your news intake.

The 24/7 news merry-go-round is depressing and causes anxiety and negative emotions. I've been without it now for months and my mornings get off to a much better start and I don't go to bed feeling depressed from the nightly news. Let's face it, there's not much you can do about it anyway.

I remember the news used to be told as a story from beginning to end and it was a mix of upbeat as well as downbeat.

Now everything is sensationalized. You get to hear the news in summary first and then comes the detail. If you forget to switch it off, at least switch it off after the headlines.

Try it and you will soon see you aren't missing much and you'll feel a lot better. If there's anything important going on, people will tell you anyway.

So, **turn off the TV news** or switch channels as soon as the news comes on.

Habit 2

Stop Reading Newspapers

A good friend of mine gets a daily newspaper. She told me reading about the state of the world and all the scare stories leaves her feeling depressed and angry. She even joked it was 'slitting your wrists' time after each read. BUT she still does it.

This tells you about **the power of negative habits**. This one impacts her life, on a daily basis, colors her views and moods. Yet, like a smoker she doesn't seem able or willing to give it up.

Besides it'll **save you time** you could be using to have fun.

Habit 3

Master Your Email Habit

Go to **www.seewilly.com** and go to Readers Tools.

Download my e-book "How To Take Control Of Your Computer And Your Time" containing 90 tips, tricks and strategies to help you organize, save time and make the best use of your computer. Go to Tip 67 **'Be the Boss of Your Email'** and convert this into a habit sticker for your PC.

This one new habit will revolutioize your working day and get you feeling a whole lot better. You'll find many of the other tips equally useful and I'm providing this free just for my readers.

Habit 4

Brush Teeth With Your Other Hand!

Here's a good way to demonstrate the power of physical habits and how you can change them, even when they are ingrained. I bet you can't imagine using your other hand to clean your teeth.

I want you to **put the habit on your bathroom mirror** so you always use the other hand for 28 days. You'll be amazed as eventually this becomes 'normal'.

Habit 5

Hang Keys Up

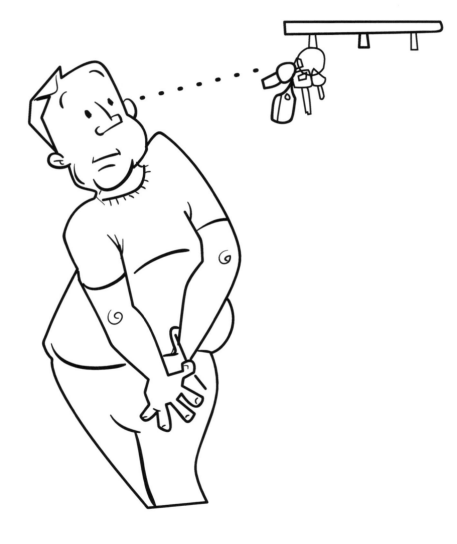

Most of us aren't as organized as we'd like to be. Get into the habit of **hanging your keys** in a set place each night. Give yourself a spot, hang a nail. Just do something. Keep up with this every time you walk in the door. Before too much longer, you'll have **a habit that can even preserve your sanity**. After all, there's nothing worse than frantically looking for keys when you're late for work!

Habit 6

Sleep On The Other Side Of The Bed

We all seem to **sleep on one side of the bed** or the other. Break this habit by creating a new one. (If your significant other will go along with this, of course). This is an easy and relatively painless new habit to form. It **will show you just how powerful habits are**.

Habit 7

Turn The Lights Off

Many of us are in the habit of leaving lights on until they burn out (practically). Form a new habit that's easy (and can save you money) by **consciously turning the lights off** each time you leave a room. Put your habit sticky on the kitchen light switch. Pretty soon you'll extend this habit to all your rooms.

Habit 8

Look Into People's Eyes

Look into people's eyes
when you are talking to them for at least
30 seconds, without looking away. You
will find this very uncomfortable to start
with, but eventually you will see it has
**a positive effect on
people**. It will also serve to increase
your own self-confidence!

Habit 9

Form A New Path To Work

Humans are creatures of habit. This extends so much into our lives that many of us go to work exactly the same way every day. **Plot a new course** and make this your new habit instead.

Habit 10

Brush Teeth After Meals

Most of us brush our teeth in the morning and at night. Our dentists will say that having just 2 teeth-cleaning habits is not enough. Make a new one by **adding a post-lunch brushing** into your routine. It's easy and your teeth might just thank you for it!

Chapter Seven

Eating, Drinking and Exercise Habits To Make You Slim

Now you've experienced the awesome power of habit, it's time to get really serious. The next 24 eating, drinking and exercise habit creators are crucial for your success.

You need to use some additional strategies now, as these new habits need to overwhelm and replace your old very powerful ones. So here goes!

First, go to the Habit list at the end of the book or download it from the Readers Tools page at the website **www.seewilly.com**. Tear off each one or re-write them onto individual Post It notes. You will need to have these in front of you at the time of habit building each and every time for at least 28 days. So once you have selected your first 2 from each of these 3 sections to work with, diary your start and end date to be sure not to miss a day. Make a note on each Post It note of start and end dates as well.

Then you need to ensure that each sticky note will be seen by you the moment you go to perform your existing habit. E.g. I have 12 stairs up to my studio at home. I had a sticky pinned to the bottom stair for 28 days saying:

RUN UP STAIRS

Start Jan 12 - End Jan 30

I made certain to do this without fail, not just once a day but every time I went up the stairs. Now a year later and with no note, I automatically run up the stairs. In fact the habit has become so ingrained I often run up ANY stairs that I go up!

To repeat - building new habits is about repetition for as long as it takes to become automatic and unthinking. Usually this is around 28 days, but can be more or less. It has nothing to do with logic, feelings, wishful thinking or anything else. Your subconscious simply needs re-programming in the most basic of ways.

If some habits seem too difficult to deal with at once, then split them up to 1 at a time and don't attempt them together. e.g. Don't eat a starter and don't eat a pudding. Wait until you are comfortably into the habit of not ordering a starter, only then tackle the pudding habit.

Remove your habit stickers on the end date and keep them. Diary a reminder to check your new habits are still working for you in 14 days time. If you missed any or they simply are not working, put the stickers back with a new end date another 28 days ahead. This will almost certainly crack it for you.

Dealing With Embarrassment

Bearing in mind you are setting yourself up for some ridicule from people (who will go on to respect and envy your commitment and achievement), you need to be prepared to handle this. Otherwise you are setting yourself up to fail. So let's consider how this is likely to crop up and ways for you to handle them.

The most effective way I have found is to use humor. So eating in a restaurant with friends, you might hear, "Come on Paul, join us in a dessert, the ice cream is fantastic", "Hurry up Paul, we've all finished, you're so slow when you eat" plus a few more. Some comments have nothing more behind them than irritation (everyone's always in a hurry), some will be meant to unsettle you and get you to weaken so you won't be seen as better than them.

Here's the trick. BEFORE you eat with anyone, if you anticipate negative reactions, make an announcement and ask people for their support. Tell them a story to make them laugh.

"You went to your doctor today for an examination for a very serious complaint. You'd lost sight of a part of your body and without the aid of mirrors you wondered if your willy had dropped off!

Apart from seeing your pee stream out from your body, your enormous belly was all to be seen. Would he please examine you to confirm your willy was still there. Relief! You passed the exam, but your doctor diagnosed you with seewillylackofitus syndrome! And if I ever want to see my willy again without the aid or a harness or mirrors, I have to follow some really new habits. So if I eat slowly or not as much or leave some food or generally do some crazy things, I'm sorry. Will you support me and my willy please?"

Or any other humorous story you can think of.

Then tell this to them before you next share a meal.

Then don't make anything of your new behavior at meals together. If they talk about it, just say you are still suffering from seewillylackofitus syndrome (until of course you get to see your willy again!).

I want you to apply the same lessons using these habits as you have before. BUT there are situations where it's not practical to use sticky notes so you need to be creative.

Memory Movies

Start by breaking down the habits you want to change in any given situation. Let's say for example, eating out. Then create the most off-the-wall crazy scenario to play in your head to remind you at the time.

Here's a fantasy movie I play to myself in my head as I walk into any restaurant or sit down to any meal. It works a treat. Feel free to adjust it for yourself or make your own, but it must be visual and memorable so there is no chance you'll forget it. And you must give yourself time for it to fully play out before you go in.

This is the scene I play in my head.

The scene is slow motion

I'm very slim wearing sexy lycra shorts I'm in a very hot dessert

I'm racing a tortoise across the sand at his (very slow pace) towards a camel in the distance

I'm parched and desperate for water

Friends are lining our route holding out plates of starters and puddings for us

They make me feel sick and I just want water, so

I slowly punch each one with first the left and then the right arm as I race and the food goes flying

A sad-looking emancipated camel appears before me - he has 2 humps

He flips open 1 hump to reveal a glass of water I drink it very slowly and gratefully and feel sorry he is so thin. He flips open the other hump to reveal a very large plated meal. I feel love for him, so I split the meal in 2 on the plate. I eat one half and leave the other on the plate for him The camel gives me a wink.

End of movie.

I sit down to my meal.

I say no to a starter and pudding and ask for water to sip all the time.

I split my meal in two and leave half for my camel to come and get later.

Play your own memory movies wherever a sticky note isn't appropriate for you. You are building your new habit reminders into your movie.

You'll slim down in no time and pretty soon you will find the thought of eating the foods you now crave a real turn-off.

EATING HABITS

Habit 11

Use A Smaller Dinner Plate

Dinner is the last meal of the day and it's an important one, but it doesn't need to be a 10-course undertaking. Keep your evening meal small and **watch the portions**. Remember, you're likely to turn in shortly after dinner. If you have too much in your stomach before you do, **your body will have a hard time working it off** during your most sedentary time of the day.

Try substituting a small side plate for your normal large dinner plate. This works wonders. You can apply this to your cereal bowl as well. Use a small soup bowl instead. Place a sticky note on your plates cupboard.

Habit 12

Drink Water - Slowly

This is **the most important HABIT** you'll get when you're trying to lose weight and slim down. When eating out, always say **yes to the water** and do drink it up. But drink it slowly so it not only fills you up, but it also fills in the time and focus that other people are using to binge on bread, starters and puddings. Water can help you **feel fuller faster** and assist you in saying no to extra portions and courses. Place a sticky note or a sticky coloured dot on your drinking tap or any bottles of water to remind you each time you pour a glass.

Habit 13

Wear Clothes That Fit

Getting into shape is a process that will become an ingrained habit over time. As you do so, your clothes will begin to sag a bit. **Don't wear pants and shirts that don't fit** you right now. If you go too tight with your clothes, you'll feel discouraged. If you leave your baggy clothes in your wardrobe, no one will be able to see the difference! **Boost your self-esteem by making "dressing right" a habit**.

Habit 14

Eat A Healthy Snack Before You Go

Munch fresh fruits or vegetables before you head out to a restaurant. When you give yourself a healthy pick-me-up a short while before you sit down to eat, you **won't be quite as hungry** and your eyes might not wander as quickly and as firmly to parts of the menu you should avoid.

Habit 15

Reduce Portion Sizes

That giant plate of pasta might look incredible, but the chances are it's enough to serve two or three. Restaurants are notorious for giving portions that are way out of whack. **You don't have to eat it all**. Really, you don't! Make a habit of leaving behind just a little from each course and before too long, you will find you can get by without wiping your plate clean.

Start by **measuring out 1/4 of your food** and put it to one side of your plate. Then leave it. Say you are full if you feel awkward leaving food on the plate. When you have made this a habit, **measure 1/2 and leave it**. You feel full but not bloated. Honestly! It's cheaper of course to just order from the kids' menu. Always remember, all the food eventually ends up in the same place anyway.

I now buy one portion of fish and chips from the chip shop and share it with my other half. We can't imagine being able to eat a whole portion each anymore. We enjoy it and feel full as well.

So make a memory movie to play back every time a large plate of food is served to you.

Habit 16

Skip Bread

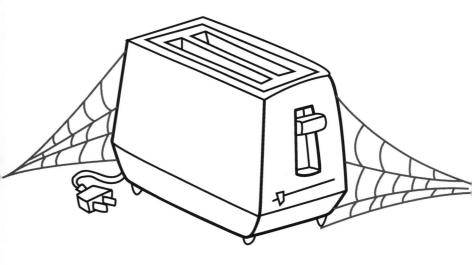

It's smart to keep carbohydrates in your diet, but it's not smart to load up on them. **Moderation is the key** here. When you're out and about and dining in a restaurant, chances are if you do have a starter it will come with carbs or starch.

Spare your stomach too much filling up by just **saying NO to the bread**. This is just designed to fill you up and it can interfere with your enjoyment of the main course.

You'll also loose more weight if you skip bread altogether at home. See some of the supporting habits for ideas.

Make this part of your restaurant memory movie.

Habit 17

Don't Skip Breakfast

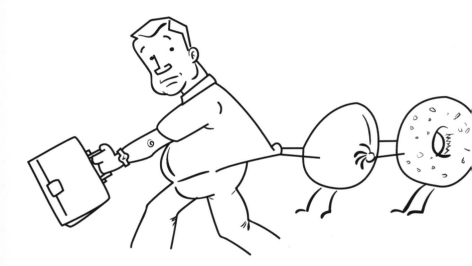

When you're trying to lose weight, skipping breakfast can seem like a smart thing to do. It's not! While busy people get out of the habit of eating the first meal of the day, this can be a huge mistake. Take the time to at least have some fresh fruit, a wholegrain bagel or something. **Put a little bit of food in your stomach** and your calorie burning processes will start off on the right foot for the whole day. No, you don't have to eat a meal fit for a king every morning.

A little can go a long way.

Habit 18

No Food After A Set Time

Some of the worst binge eating happens to take place in the evening hours after dinner. It's just so tempting to sit down and watch a movie or game show on the TV and snack away. To get yourself into the swing of being healthier, **set a time to cut off eating** and stick with it. If you turn in around 11 p.m., cut off foods at 8. Place a sticky on your fridge or larder. If you are really hungry drink some water slowly.

Habit 19

Eat Slowly - Focus On Each Mouthful

Usually, people eating together tend to eat at the same pace. This tends to be the pace of the quickest eater. Make it your habit to completely **ignore how other people are eating** or gorging around you. Focus on your own plate of food. Take one mouthful and put your knife and fork down. Think about the food you are eating and **chew it slowly and thoroughly**. This will aid digestion and your stomach will feel fuller with less. Then pick up your knife and fork and repeat the process.

Habit 20

Choose The Restaurant

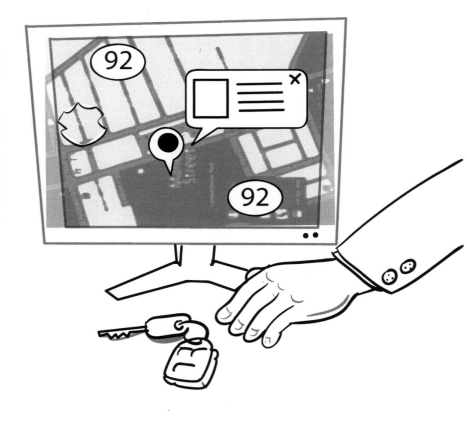

Be the decisive one when it's time to eat out - you can do it! Pick places that offer tasty, but healthy foods that appeal. This will help you stay on track and can assist you in developing another smart habit - **avoiding places** that don't have healthy foods on the menu.

DRINKING HABITS

A couple of pints or a few glasses of wine are the same as eating a whole carrot cake! But let's face it, who cares. We use our drinking to relax and unwind so surely this is going to be REALLY hard to do.

Not so! Just remember your drinking habits rule you as much as your eating habits do. They are familiar and comfortable. You'll be using the power of habits to make your new drinking habits just as, if not more, enjoyable. You're just finding that hard to imagine right now.

Remember you don't really need to 'imagine'. You just need to reprogram yourself. Once you have new habits in place, you'll still enjoy a drink just as much, but you won't feel so tired afterwards and of course, when you go to the urinal you'll be smiling at the sight of your long lost friend!

It's going to be easy getting these habits at home, but if you are like me and enjoy a drink or two in the pub, Post-it notes won't cut it!

In this case choose 2 habits at a time and master them from the list below. An example would be to use my desert movie, but replace the starters being held out by friends to be large pints, peanuts and crisps. The camel humps will contain a half pint of lager or beer or a small glass of wine, and the other hump has a glass of water. Make up your own 'drinking' movie. The stranger and weirder the better as this will be more memorable. Remember, you are the only one watching it.

Once you've mastered these 2/3 habits, make a new movie to cover the rest.

Habit 21

Drink Half Pints - And Slowly

Pace yourself so you finish your half at the same time others finish a pint. If you are embarrassed at a half pint of beer in a small glass, **switch to a bottled beer** instead and say you now prefer that to draught. Always ask for a half-pint glass of tap water to alternate with at the same time.

Habit 22

Drink Small Glasses Of Wine

Many pubs and bars only offer large glasses nowadays, so **insist on a smaller measure**. Drink it **slowly** to match the speed of people who are drinking much larger measures.

Habit 23

Focus On Sipping - Not Drinking

Use a **small sticky dot** or cut a tiny sticky dot from a Post It note. Have these in your wallet and **incorporate their use into your memory movie**. So when you go into the pub, stick one to your drinking hand thumbnail. This **will remind you everytime** you lift a glass to drink, to slow down, focus and sip slowly instead.

Habit 24

Skip Crisps And Nuts

There's **more fat** in these than in some main meals. If you are feeling peckish ask for a **healthy snack** or better still **drink water** instead.

EXERCISE HABITS

You can slim down successfully by building the eating and drinking habits. But why stop there?

In just the same way you couldn't imagine doing without a pudding or the whole bottle of wine; you'll be even more skeptical about exercise.

Well I was too. Here's how I created just a few exercise habits that not only helped me slim, they literally changed my life. You see the benefits of exercise are many, mostly to do with good health and avoiding diseases. For me, getting moving helped my motivation and always helped to lift my mood on grey winters days.

I used my Post-it notes in my home to get me into the habit of running up stairs (now I start to run at any stairs I see). I started to walk short distances instead of driving. With my belly fast disappearing without the 'familiar' bloated and tired feelings my old eating and drinking habits had saddled me with, I felt free to increase my exercise even more. I experimented with aerobic exercise at my local gym, but then realized I could more easily just run for part of my walking instead. Unbelievably I have run my first 6-mile charity race and I've enjoyed it so much, I'll be sticking with it.

Not long ago, I couldn't run 50 yards without collapsing out of breath and unable to lift my legs all the time. Now, anything is possible!

I'm not suggesting you join a gym or start running. Just start out and build a few new exercise habits for life. You'll not only accelerate your slimming down, you'll feel better and you'll probably live longer!

So, use Post-it notes where you can, and where you can't, make a mental movie. Funny, crazy, whatever. As long as you remember it and play it every day. Use a Post-it note on the outside of the shower. Then you can relax and play your movie while showering.

Habit 25

Take The Stairs

Want to watch pounds melt away without ever really feeling like you've done much to achieve the goal?

Take the stairs at work or at home rather than using the lift. If you have to get up and down a lot during the day or night, this will add up fast to a real workout.

Better still **run up stairs** for even better effect. Pin a Post-it note to your stairs with start and end dates as usual. When you run up them as a habit, you'll automatically apply this to stairs outside the home.

Habit 26

Stand Up

Whenever it's at all possible, **stand up rather than sit down**. This will enable you to move around a bit more and you can burn some additional calories along the way.

See Willy®

Habit 27

Move During Commercials

If you love to settle in and watch a little television in the evenings, don't let the time be wasted on the exercise front. Use Post-it notes on your TV or remote control. **Get up and move around** during the commercials. Stretch your legs a bit. Do some jumping jacks. **Just do something!**

Habit 28

Use A Cordless Phone

If you spend a lot of time on the phone, put that time to good use! **Get a cordless phone** and walk around the office or the house when you're busy in conversation. This is a great way to keep yourself moving and stretched out and it can **burn a calorie or two extra along the way**.

Habit 29

Get An Office Alarm Clock

If you have to sit at a desk all day, **get an alarm clock** to work for you. Set it to go off **every 30 minutes**. If you are using a computer go to Google and search for '"free alarm clock" and install one. Set your alarm and when it goes off, get up and move around a bit. You'll feel better and you'll burn some calories in the process.

While you do this, organize your workspace to remove barriers to being able to relax and exercise.

Habit 30

Do Chair Exercises

Believe it or not, you can **burn some serious calories** while sitting in your chair at work. Develop a basic routine of chair exercises to keep yourself in shape even when you can't get up.

The best place to see chair exercises is at www.youtube.com. Simply enter "chair exercises" in the search box.

Habit 31

Walk To Work

If you don't live too far away, get into the habit of **walking to work**. If you commute or take public transport, **get off early and walk the rest**. With the price of fuel likely to be going up and up, your wallet will thank you as much for this one as your waist will.

Habit 32

Get A Pedometer

Buy a pedometer (they cost very little) and use it! Aim to **walk at least 10,000 steps a day**. You'll be surprised at just how quickly this can happen, too. Taking the stairs, walking to work and moving around during commercial breaks at night will add up extra paces.

Habit 33

Park Further Away From Your Home Or Office

Stake out a parking space that's **a little farther away** from the front door to force you to **walk a little further**. Every step counts when it comes to getting into shape.

Habit 34

Take Stairs 2 At A Time

If you're coordinated enough to pull this off, it's a great habit to develop. Not only is taking the stairs healthier and smarter, but it can get your heart pumping. **Taking them two at a time** can increase the workout aspect of the climb.

AND
THE REST

SUPPORTING HABITS

I've kept your new power habits to the minimum. Too many will put you off and too few will be ineffective. There are plenty of other good habits and general actions you can consider, and these will support you in your quest to see willy.

Browse this section and try to adopt just a few at time if you feel you can handle them. If it all seems too much, wait until you have established some new habits from the first sections before adopting these.

Come up with ways to have your "auto response" working when you need it with a Post-it note or a mental movie, or just diary it as an action to do e.g. "Book a drumming lesson".

Habit 35

Don't Clean Your Plate

Forget what your mother told you. Starving children won't go hungry if you don't eat everything on your plate. Just because a "serving" is huge doesn't mean you need to eat the whole thing. In fact, you're going to discover that **properly portioned servings** are a whole lot smaller than what we normally dish out for ourselves.

Try to ease yourself into eating "just enough" rather than "too much." Before too long, you'll have the hang of it!

The habit you want to develop here is nothing more than eating **until you're comfortable** - not stuffed!

Habit 36

Count When You Chew

A friend of mine swears by mentally counting to nine or 10 every time she puts a bite of food into her mouth. This helps her remember to **slow down and properly chew** her food before she swallows.

Getting started on this one will be a bit awkward, but it can really help you control your portions and food intake. The longer you take to chew, the more likely it is that "full" message will make it to your brain before you eat more than you need to or really should.

Habit 37

Focus On How You Eat

Pay attention to what you do when you eat. Chances are you eat fast out of fear someone might just take your plate away before you're done! Instead of worrying about the second slice of bread, zero in on what's in front of you and **try to eat slowly and chew your food properly**. I know this sounds like something your Mother would say, but eating slowly and chewing correctly can help you eat less. Your body will have the time it needs to digest and actually realize that it's full. Don't worry, eating less doesn't mean starving yourself to death.

Habit 38

Picture Your Last Meal In Detail

Before you dive into your present meal, consider carefully **everything you ate the last time you did**. The mental imagery can help you better focus on how much you've already had to eat today and can guide you in making a subconscious decision to eat a little less during your current meal.

Take the time to carefully **picture every morsel** and you'll turn this little practice into a habit in no time at all.

Habit 39

Say "No" To Dessert

The dessert menu used to be a nightmare of mine. It is, after all, terribly **difficult to say no** to a giant piece of chocolate cake that just rolls right by your table. **Learn to say no**. Make it a habit. If I can do it, so can you. If you must indulge, reserve doing so for special occasions and even consider splitting a dessert with others at the table.

Habit 40

Consider What You Can Add To Your Diet

Focus on the 5 portions of fruit and vegetables each day. You are less likely to overeat as you feel more satisfied from the volume of food. Plus you are getting more essential fiber that's **good for your digestive system**.

Habit 41

Set Your Alarm Clock 5 Minutes Earlier

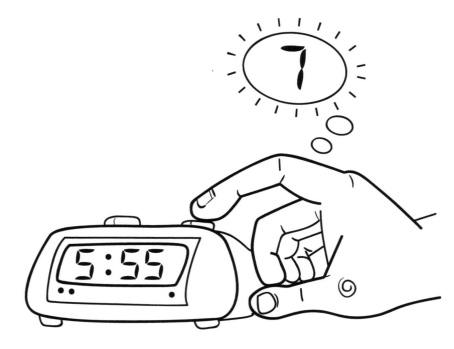

If your excuse for not eating breakfast or drinking fluids in the morning involves a lack of time, give yourself some! When you have grab-and-go foods on hand, it only takes five minutes or less to remedy the "no time" problem. Get into the habit of setting your alarm clock **just five or 10 minutes ealier** and you'll free up plenty of seconds to get in a quick meal and a glass of water.

Habit 42

Drink Calorie-free Drinks

Before snacking, Check whether you are just thirsty and not actually hungry. No sense is taking in excess calories when all you need is a drink. Then **take plain water or add a little juice**. If you've never tried black tea or fruit tea, now would be a good time.

Habit 43

Eat Several Small Snacks A Day

When you are hungry all the time, eating less is very hard. As you are reducing your main meal portions, eat several low calorie snacks a day to **keep your metabolism going** and give you the energy you need.

Habit 44

Drink 6 Glasses Of Water - Slowly

Don't forget to keep yourself hydrated during the day. A few glasses of **water after breakfast** and during lunch can help you feel full and assist you in steering clear of snacks that won't help your mission.

Habit 45

Avoid The Diet Wreckers

Some foods you think are healthy are packed with calories, carbs or starch. So avoid caesar salad, fresh smoothies that use concentrates, most energy bars, breakfast muffins, bread, fried foods, low fat yogurt (high in sugar), anything labelled 'light', coleslaw. Use a sticky note on your shopping trolley to remind you to **check everything you buy** for sugar and fat content. You'll be amazed and shocked at what you discover!

Habit 46

No Sweets On The Desk

It's an all too common habit in many offices to have a desk or two that's the "sweet stop." Make sure this isn't your desk. If it is, **break the habit** of hosting the sweets stash personally by moving it to a more centralized location.

Habit 47

Avoid The "Snack Area"

Provided your desk isn't the sweets or snack stop in the office make a point of **avoiding the desk** where it's stored. You can bolster your will power to say no to walk-and-grab snacks by simply avoiding them.

Do make a point of saying hello to the co-worker who hosts the snack desk though ... you wouldn't want him or her to think you're avoiding them! Make it clear it's **just the snacks you're trying to break up with!**

Habit 48

Don't Skip Lunch

When you're trying to lose weight and time in the office is at a premium, skipping lunch might seem like a good idea. It's not! You do need **a decent afternoon meal** to keep your body energized and ready to tackle the rest of the day. You don't, however, need to pig out. **Smaller portions** will leave you feeling better and give you the energy you need to plough through until 5 or 6.

Habit 49

Snack Wisely When You Get Home

If dinner isn't on the table when you walk through the door (and really, in today's world, who has the ability to make it so?), eat a **small quick snack** when you walk in. A healthy and tasty snack will brace you to wait for dinner and will prevent you from munching on everything in sight while you prepare the meal. **Alternatively drink water** to help you feel full.

Habit 50

Make Dinner A Priority

Skipping dinner is one of the worst things you can do for developing healthier habits that last. Pass up on this meal and you're likely to find yourself with a bag of chips in hand later in the evening. **Dinner doesn't have to be huge** to be effective though.

Habit 51

Have Dressings Served On The Side

Believe it or not those special sauces, dips, dressings and toppings can add up to a huge amount in a calorie count. Since we don't count calories, getting into the habit of having them served on the side can help you portion out only what you need for taste.   Before too long, you'll discover you don't   have   to   slather everything with condiments to enjoy some incredible flavor in your food. You might even **rediscover** what foods like meat and vegetables **taste** like on   their   own. They're not half bad. Really!

Habit 52

Keep Dinner Balanced

Make sure your **food group bases are covered** at dinner (and all other meals, too). You don't really need more than a basic meat, vegetable and starch at dinnertime. Get into the habit of covering the bases and you're likely to discover you feel better, look better and can live without a fast-food snack.

Habit 53

Plan Meals Ahead

I know it's hard to plan meals. But, if you don't have someone to do it for you, **planning a menu ahead of time** and sticking with it can keep you out of fast-food establishments at dinner time.

Habit 54

Cook Dinner Ahead

Dinner can be one of the most dangerous meals of the day. The fact is after a hard day of working, the last thing you want to do is come home and cook. To prevent the urge to pick up a take-out instead, try **cooking meals ahead of time**.

Stake out Sundays, for example, as your cooking day. Freeze meals for easy reheating. **Cook 2 meals at the same time**. Eat one and freeze the other.

Habit 55

Skip Dessert

Eating dessert with dinner is a habit in many homes. Break this if it's a habit in yours! Instead, try **snacking on fresh fruits** or other "healthy" sweets later in the evening. Keep the cake, pie, cookies and other junk foods reserved for special occasions. If you learn to say no, it will become a habit you can live with.

Habit 56

Skip The Starters

They might be oh so tempting, but starters can pack quite the punch when it comes to extra calories added to a meal. Learn to **just say no** and you'll have more room to **enjoy your main meal** comfortably. There's no reason to stuff yourself to death just because you're at a restaurant. If you must have the starters, go for a smaller, lighter dish for the main course, or skip the main course all together.

Habit 57

Do A Night Time Routine

If you get yourself into the habit of doing something fun or personally rewarding at night, you'll be less likely to snack on treats during the dangerous evening hours.

Try creating a routine that **involves physical activities** for an even bigger impact. Anything **from having sex to walking the dog**. Make a memory movie to play every evening. Go to the Readers Tools area of the website **www.seewilly.com** for more examples of memory movies you can use or adapt.

Habit 58

Drink Water At Night

No, you don't want to float yourself before you turn in! Still, **a glass of water or two in the evening** can keep you feeling more full and help you avoid those nasty night time snacks.

Habit 59

Replace Fat Filled Snacks With Healthy Convenience Foods

Stock up with ready-to-eat meals and ingredients you can use in minutes. Pre-cooked chicken, tinned tomatoes, brown rice, vegetables are just some ideas. Buy yourself a book on stir fry cooking for other **quick healthy and filling meals**.

Habit 60

Limit Alcohol In The Evening

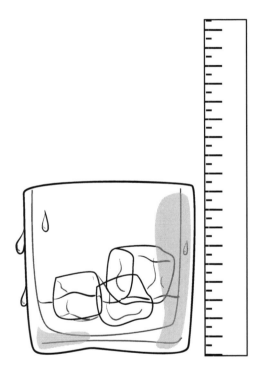

This is a "hidden" calorie pitfall that we just seem to fall into all the time. Yes, it's hard to say no to a glass of wine or beer in the evening, however those nightly alcoholic drinks can pack a massive punch on the calorie front!

Limit intake to one or learn to skip an evening drink entirely to keep on the right track. Alcohol tends to be very high in calories and wine and **beer is loaded with carbs**.

Habit 61

Order Off Kids' Menu

A friend of mine likes to eat out with his kids - a lot. He noticed that the kids portions were rather large for their tastes, but were quite **ideal for an adult**. Not only are kids menus loaded with the same dishes that adults are served, they're **cheaper, too**. There's no reason why you can't lose weight and be frugal, too!

Habit 62

Meditate

Give yourself a few minutes of **quiet time each day** to reflect on your goals, your progress and where you'd like to see yourself in a month, year or five more years down the road. Go over your successes in your mind and **pinpoint areas you need to work on**.

Habit 63

Visualize

Mentally picture yourself achieving your goals in life. When you see yourself doing something, you can make it reality!

Habit 64

Celebrate Success!

We all spend too much time dwelling on our failures and not enough celebrating the little successes we enjoy in life. When you **reach a goal** (even a tiny one), there's cause to **celebrate**. Just do it!

Habit 65

Flirt!

As you reshape yourself and your life to become the person you want to be, don't be afraid to **show it off a little**. If you have a significant other in your life, have some fun flirting with them If you don't, show off your new found self by **flirting** with others!

Habit 66

Be Kind To Me

Make it a point to acknowledge something **about yourself that you like** each day. It doesn't matter what it is, just **recognize and appreciate** that you have achieved a goal, have special talents or can do something better than anyone else you know.

Habit 67

Be Kind To Others

If you really want to feel good about yourself deep down, make it a habit to **be nice to others**. When you put smiles on your loved ones' faces or those of strangers, you will **feel better about yourself** and life in general.

Habit 68

Get Up And Get It Myself

If you have a bad habit of asking others to do things for you that you could do yourself, stop it! **Don't ask someone else** to grab you a drink, a snack or the newspaper on the table that's two feet away.

Habit 69

Be Grateful

Count your blessings and be grateful. Your quest to see your willy is an important one, but **keep it in perspective**. Use a sticky note at your bedside so you wake up feeling grateful everyday.

Habit 70

Water Down Coffee

Take what you've learned about breaking and forming habits and apply it to other areas of your life. If you are hooked on caffeine, for example, learn to kick that habit by just **watering it down**. You can wean yourself quickly by adding a little water to your coffee or tea. Add a little more every day and before too much longer you will find you can **do without your daily fix**. Use a sticky note at the coffee making area.

Habit 71

Get Organized

Stress is one factor that can quickly undo all your good habits and turn them bad. To avoid unnecessary stress, organize your life. **Get one calendar and stick with it**. Clean out your desk at work. Tidy up your home. When you have a little **control over your surroundings**, stress is less likely to hit you like a truck. My e-book "How To Take Control Of Your Computer and Your Time" is packed with ideas and strategies you can use. Download it for free at the Readers Tools area at **www.seewilly.com** while you think about it.

Habit 72

Eat Sandwiches With 1 Slice Of Bread

Cutting out bread will accelerate your weight loss, so start by cutting down. **Take the top layer of bread off** your sandwiches and leave it. Do the same with burgers. Take off the top half of the bap and leave it.

Habit 73

Laugh!

Believe it or not, **laughing can burn more calories** than sitting around frowning. Watch comedies, play with a kid ... just do something to enjoy a few good belly laughs a day. Google "jokes" on the Internet and start honing your joke-telling skills! Use a sticky note to remind yourself to review the number of times you remember laughing every day. Then simply increase your laugh time.

Habit 74

Hug!

Take the time to **cuddle, hug and touch** the people you love the most. This feels great and can burn a few calories along the way. You'll feel better, they'll feel better and **everyone will be calmer and happier!** Make a memory movie to follow each time you meet someone that it's appropriate to hug. Imagine the warm feelings for both of you and pretty soon it'll become one of your favourite habits.

Habit 75

Walk A Dog

If you want a great workout, **take your dog out for a walk or run**. If you don't have a dog, borrow one! You and Fido will have a blast walking around a block or through the woods and you can get a serious workout (especially if he spots a cat along the way.)

Habit 76

Learn To Dance

Who said "exercise" can't have rhythm? If you want to enjoy an excellent workout that doesn't feel like one, **take up dancing**. This is a great way to shape up, lose fat and have a great time all at once.

Habit 77

Do Shower Exercises

If you don't want anyone to see you while you're exercising, the **shower is a great place to go**. At the very least, take advantage of a nice hot shower to **start your stretching** exercises. The warm water can help you relax. Before you know it, you will be able to touch your toes! Use a sticky note on the shower to help you build the habit.

Habit 78

Park An Exercise Machine In Front Of TV

You can watch your favorite show and get a great workout at the same time! When you **park an exercise bike** or treadmill in front of the television, you won't even know you're exercising when you are. **Start out slow** with half-hour sessions in front of your favourite sit-com.

After you get into the swing of it, work up to full one-hour shows. (Take breaks to walk and stretch during the commercials.)

Habit 79

Teach A Child To Play Ball

If you have kids, **get out and play** with them for a workout with serious meaning. If you don't have a kid to play with, **borrow one!**

Habit 80

Take Up A Sport

Exercise doesn't have to be boring! **Take up a sport** you've always wanted to try to enjoy a great cardiovascular workout that's challenging. Golfing, swimming, tennis, football, soccer and more can all **work wonders**.

Habit 81

Do Gardening

Gardening is exercise!

If you don't believe it, try weeding, mulching and planting your back garden. You'll break out in a sweat in no time at all.

Heavy gardening on a regular basis does add up to a **fantastic workout** and it can make your property value soar in the process.

Habit 82

Bike To Shops

When it's time to pick up a few things, **leave the car at home** and pull out a bike with a luggage rack instead. This is a great way to pick up a few days' worth of groceries and **burn some calories** in the process.

Habit 83

Beat Out Frustrations

Put up a **punch bag** in your garage or spare room. Practice your boxing on a regular basis to work out and you'll find your **frustrations and stress melt away**, too.

Habit 84

Walk Up And Down Escalators

When you're out and about and stairs aren't an option, **be creative** in working in a little exercise.

Walk up or down an escalator if it's an option instead of taking the lift or elevator. Don't try this on a packed escalator, but if you have a clear path, it's a great way to add on a few steps to your day.

Habit 85

Have More Sex

Of all the ways to exercise, this one might be the most enjoyable. Believe it or not, sex can be a **fantastic workout** that both you and your partner will enjoy. Get into the habit of setting aside a little more "alone time" on a regular basis and you'll burn plenty of extra calories in the process. As you develop other healthy habits and reach your goal of being able to see Willy, you'll find this particular "habit" becomes **even more enjoyable, too!**

Habit 86

Learn To Play The Drums

Playing drums is one of the best ways I know to **work up a sweat** and have fun. Don't worry if you think you could never do this. Just call up a local drumming teacher and get going. Use an electronic kit with headphones if you are worried about annoying your neighbors.

SOME CLOSING TIPS

Losing weight on a full stomach

People assume the quickest way to loose weight is to skip meals and therefore skip calories, but it doesn't work.

Good thinking and eating habits and keeping full are what does.

According to recent research, when your stomach is empty your brain is stimulated to produce the ghrelin hormone giving rise to an increase in appetite and in particular by the need for high calorie foods.

This happens unconsciously, it's not a matter of will power. The unconscious part of your brain then zeros in on high calorie food.

This has been proved by showing hungry people pictures of high calorie food and salads and measuring brain activity using MRI scanners.

Guess what? Salads do nothing for appetite brain activity. So, when you are full, your brain is not activated to want more food.

The trick then is to never be hungry. To fill up on low calorie foods so your brain won't get the ghrelin hormone and start you craving for high calorie foods.

Two powerful ways to achieve this were measured on men working on physical tasks.

Protein for breakfast. Adding 10% of protein at breakfast time meant they could go much longer before hunger set in. So if you have a cooked breakfast add some beans to your eggs and ham.

Soup keeps you fuller for longer. At lunchtime, some men were given a meal whilst others were given the same but it was liquidized into a soup. The men who had the soup went far longer before hunger set in. Soup takes longer for the stomach to act on it and therefore the stomach stays fuller for longer.

Low fat dairy helps. Milk and cheese are often given up on diets. However the recommended daily content of calcium in these foods reaches your intestine and binds to fat and moves the fat straight through you. A high calcium diet can excrete double the amount of fat. Therefore low fat dairy food may help. Skimmed milk, low fat cottage cheese, crème fresh, low fat yogurt.

Don't kid yourself! There is no such thing as suffering a low metabolic rate and putting weight on as a result. Tests with detailed eating diaries showed people simply eat too much and eat too much high calorie food. They under reported what they eat by as much as 50%!

Just take a couple of items you tend to consume and be aware of some changes you could make. E.g.

Hidden calories are not obvious. A tiny chocolate = a large sandwich.

Black coffee had 10 calories = cappuccino has 100 calories 3 black coffees a day saves 270 calories.

A slice of toast 125 calories = pastry 270 calories.

Lunch of chicken salad with vinaigrette 250 calories = the same with mozzarella and mayo 450 calories.

3 apples 120 calories = bar of chocolate 300 calories.

Pizza and cocktails 850 calories = deep pan pepperoni 1,400 calories.

So fill up on low calorie foods so you can stay full for longer.

Your Personal Plan

You now know the true power of "Habit". You have seen how this power has been ruling and ruining your life. In this book I have provided you with the means to ditch old habits and re-program your life with powerful, positive and happy new ones.

The reality is, you only need to create a small number of the habits in this book and you will start to experience weight dropping away to reveal a new slim and fitter you.

Since everyone is different, you should take your time now to review the information and habits and make a small starting list to work with.

It's going to be crucial to limit this to just 2 or 3 at a time from each section and see them through into everyday habits before you move on and take on more habits.

If you take on too many new habits in one go, you will fail in a confusion of sticky notes and memory movies. You will lose your commitment and you will have lost this marvellous opportunity.

So, please re-read the introductory sections and write up your own plan now. Decide how you are going to use sticky notes and practise your memory movies. Then get going.

Finally

This book is more than what you are holding.

I wanted to include more information for you, more tips and strategies and more support material, but it's not possible to include it all.

So please visit the website www.seewilly.com and go to the Readers Only Tools area. You'll be asked to enter a password from this book so you can get free access to the readers only area.

Here are a few things you'll find there. More will be added so while you are there sign up for the free newsletter so you can get them when they become available.

How To Take Control Of Your Computer and Time ebook.

See Willy habit list that you can print out.

Memory Movie examples to use or adapt

And much more.

Don't Put This Book Away Yet!

I've read many books myself, some containing really useful ideas and plans to help me achieve my goals. Depending on what's been going on in my life at the time, I will either put the book on the shelf to work with later, or I'll re-read it and get on with it.

Guess what, I'm still discovering those great books I shelved many years later. As powerful as I felt they were at the time, everyday life took over and I never got the benefits at the time.

So, this really is your opportunity to start seeing a change around in your weight, fitness and general levels of happiness.

Well done, if you plan to start now, but please think again if you decide to "put it off" for later.

Life is for living today - here's my take on why.

I have been developing my personal weight loss techniques for many years. I had intended "one day" to take time out to write this book to help others overcome weight problems that blight their lives. But it was always on the "back burner".

Not long ago I was diagnosed with prostate cancer and like a lot of people facing a potential bleak outcome, I made my own personal commitment to take stock of the things I wanted to achieve and re-prioritize my life. I was lucky to be living the life I wanted, but there was much more to experience and achieve. You are holding one of these projects in your hands and I sincerely wish that it will help you achieve one of your own personal goals to maintain a healthy body and weight.

You'll have heard it before many times. "Life isn't a rehearsal", "Live your life to the full while you can", "Stop thinking and start living" and other similar sage advice.

None of them have a lasting impact for most people. Life has these awful "habits" of leading us along at a frenetic pace, bogged down with past guilt and anger, worrying what's around the corner while all the time missing out on living the here-and-now.

That magical moment that's really all there is. Is right here, right now.

Perhaps the time this comes into sharpest focus is when people are facing critical illness. Or when they are much older, they may look back with regret and some sadness at opportunities missed.

If today were going to be the last day of your life, would you want to live it the way you will be living it today? In the face of death all pride, embarrassment, fear of failure, fear of loss just drop away, leaving only what's really important to you.

Use this opportunity to re-assert your commitment to bringing more joy and happiness into your life by reshaping your physical body, your weight and with it increasing your confidence to live life fully.

Be bold and don't worry what anyone thinks about you.

Enjoy - Just do it!

UP AND AT EM!

Go to **www.seewilly.com** and register for instant access to my readers-only free tips, tricks, shortcuts and advice to make your journey easier.

While you are there find out how membership of the see-willy club will sky rocket your motivation, enjoyment and long-term success – all using the power of habit!

READY FOR MORE LIFE CHANGING OPPORTUNITIES?

Perhaps there are other life changes you want to make but haven't yet got around to. Check out my website for the latest simple, practical solutions at:

www.markmeakings.tv

• Mark Meakings's Stop Smoking Power Habit Book – Where I will reveal to you how to use my power habit system to help you finally kick this evil habit!

• Mark Meakings's Internet Payday System – thousands of everyday inexperienced people are learning how to generate cash online. Now it's your turn!

• Mark Meakings's KAZ 90 Minutes Typing Tutor – Yes, like over 1 million people of all ages at the Open University, schools, colleges, at work and even on QVC TV, you really can learn to touch type in just 90 minutes!

Habit 1- Stop Watching TV News !
Start Date: ....../....../........... Finish Date: ....../....../...........
Notes: ....

Habit 2 - Stop Reading Newspapers
Start Date: ....../....../........... Finish Date: ....../....../...........
Notes: ....

Habit 3 - Master Your Email Habit
Start Date: ....../....../........... Finish Date: ....../....../...........
Notes: ....

Habit 4 - Brush Teeth With Other Hand!
Start Date: ....../....../........... Finish Date: ....../....../...........
Notes: ....

Habit 5 - Hang Keys Up
Start Date: ....../....../........... Finish Date: ....../....../...........
Notes: ....

Habit 6 - Sleep On The Other Side Of the bed
Start Date: ....../....../........... Finish Date: ....../....../...........
Notes: ....

Habit 7 - Turn The Lights Off
Start Date: ....../....../........... Finish Date: ....../....../...........
Notes: ....

Habit 8 - Look Into People's Eyes
Start Date: ....../....../........... Finish Date: ....../....../...........
Notes: ....

Habit 9 - Form A New Path To Work
Start Date: ....../....../........... Finish Date: ....../....../...........
Notes: ....

Habit 10 - Brush Teeth After Meals
Start Date: ....../....../........... Finish Date: ....../....../...........
Notes: ....

Habit 11 - Use A Smaller Dinner Plate
Start Date: ....../....../........... Finish Date: ....../....../...........
Notes: ....

Habit 12 - Drink Water - Slowly
Start Date: ....../....../........... Finish Date: ....../....../...........
Notes: ....

Habit 13 - Wear Clothes That Fit
Start Date: ....../....../........... Finish Date: ....../....../...........
Notes: ....

Habit 14 - Eat A Healthy Snack Before You Go
Start Date: ....../....../........... Finish Date: ....../....../...........
Notes: ....

Habit 15 - Reduce Portion Sizes
Start Date: ....../....../........... Finish Date: ....../....../...........
Notes: ....

Habit 16 - Skip Bread
Start Date: ....../....../........... Finish Date: ....../....../...........
Notes: ....

Habit 17 - Don't Skip Breakfast
Start Date: ....../....../........... Finish Date: ....../....../...........
Notes: ....

Habit 18 - No Food After A Set Time
Start Date: ....../....../........... Finish Date: ....../....../...........
Notes: ....

Habit 19 - Eat Slowly - Focus On Each Mouthful
Start Date: ....../....../........... Finish Date: ....../....../...........
Notes: ....

Habit 20 - Choose The Restaurant
Start Date: ....../....../........... Finish Date: ....../....../...........
Notes: ....

Habit 21 - Drink Half Pints - And Slowly
Start Date: ....../....../........... Finish Date: ....../....../...........
Notes: ....

Habit 22 - Drink Small Glasses Of Wine
Start Date: ....../....../........... Finish Date: ....../....../...........
Notes: ....
....

Habit 23 - Focus On Sipping - Not Drinking
Start Date: ....../....../........... Finish Date: ....../....../...........
Notes: ....
....

Habit 24 - Skip Crisps And Nuts
Start Date: ....../....../........... Finish Date: ....../....../...........
Notes: ....
....

Habit 25 - Take The Stairs
Start Date: ....../....../........... Finish Date: ....../....../...........
Notes: ....
....

Habit 26 - Stand Up
Start Date: ....../....../........... Finish Date: ....../....../...........
Notes: ....
....

Habit 27 - Move During Commercials
Start Date: ....../....../........... Finish Date: ....../....../...........
Notes: ....
....

Habit 28 - Use A Cordless Phone
Start Date: ....../....../........... Finish Date: ....../....../...........
Notes: ....
....

Habit 29 - Get An Office Alarm Clock
Start Date: ....../....../........... Finish Date: ....../....../...........
Notes: ....

Habit 30 - Do Chair Exercises
Start Date: ....../....../........... Finish Date: ....../....../...........
Notes: ....

Habit 31 - Walk To Work
Start Date: ....../....../........... Finish Date: ....../....../...........
Notes: ....

Habit 32 - Get A Pedometer
Start Date: ....../....../........... Finish Date: ....../....../...........
Notes: ....

Habit 33 - Park Further Away...
Start Date: ....../....../........... Finish Date: ....../....../...........
Notes: ....

Habit 34 - Take Stairs 2 At A Time
Start Date: ....../....../........... Finish Date: ....../....../...........
Notes: ....

Habit 35 - Don't Clean Your Plate
Start Date: ....../....../........... Finish Date: ....../....../...........
Notes: ....

Habit 36 - Count When You Chew
Start Date: ....../....../.......... Finish Date: ....../....../..........
Notes: ....

Habit 37 - Focus On How You Eat
Start Date: ....../....../.......... Finish Date: ....../....../..........
Notes: ....

Habit 38 - Picture Your Last Meal In Detail
Start Date: ....../....../.......... Finish Date: ....../....../..........
Notes: ....

Habit 39 - Say 'No" To Dessert
Start Date: ....../....../.......... Finish Date: ....../....../..........
Notes: ....

Habit 40 - Consider What You Can Add To Your Diet
Start Date: ....../....../.......... Finish Date: ....../....../..........
Notes: ....

Habit 41 - Set Your Alarm Clock 5 Minutes Earlier
Start Date: ....../....../.......... Finish Date: ....../....../..........
Notes: ....

Habit 42 - Drink Calorie-free Drinks
Start Date: ....../....../.......... Finish Date: ....../....../..........
Notes: ....

Habit 43 - Eat Several Small Snacks A Day
Start Date: ....../....../........... Finish Date: ....../....../...........
Notes: ....

Habit 44 - Drink 6 Glasses Of Water
Start Date: ....../....../........... Finish Date: ....../....../...........
Notes: ....

Habit 45 - Avoid The Diet Wreckers
Start Date: ....../....../........... Finish Date: ....../....../...........
Notes: ....

Habit 46 - No Sweets On The Desk
Start Date: ....../....../........... Finish Date: ....../....../...........
Notes: ....

Habit 47 - Avoid The "Snack Area"
Start Date: ....../....../........... Finish Date: ....../....../...........
Notes: ....

Habit 48 - Don't Skip Lunch
Start Date: ....../....../........... Finish Date: ....../....../...........
Notes: ....

Habit 49 - Snack Wisely When You Get Home
Start Date: ....../....../........... Finish Date: ....../....../...........
Notes: ....

Habit 50 - Make Dinner A Priority
Start Date: ....../....../........... Finish Date: ....../....../...........
Notes: ....

Habit 51 - Have Dressings Served On The Side
Start Date: ....../....../........... Finish Date: ....../....../...........
Notes: ....

Habit 52 - Keep Dinner Balanced
Start Date: ....../....../........... Finish Date: ....../....../...........
Notes: ....

Habit 53 - Plan Meals Ahead
Start Date: ....../....../........... Finish Date: ....../....../...........
Notes: ....

Habit 54 - Cook Dinner Ahead
Start Date: ....../....../........... Finish Date: ....../....../...........
Notes: ....

Habit 55 - Skip Dessert
Start Date: ....../....../........... Finish Date: ....../....../...........
Notes: ....

Habit 56 - No Food After A Set Time
Start Date: ....../....../........... Finish Date: ....../....../...........
Notes: ....

Habit 57 - Do A Night Time Routine
Start Date: ....../....../........... Finish Date: ....../....../...........
Notes: ....

Habit 58 - Drink Water At Night
Start Date: ....../....../........... Finish Date: ....../....../...........
Notes: ....

Habit 59 - Replace Fat Filled Snacks
Start Date: ....../....../........... Finish Date: ....../....../...........
Notes: ....

Habit 60 - Limit Alcohol In The Evening
Start Date: ....../....../........... Finish Date: ....../....../...........
Notes: ....

Habit 61 - Order Off The Kids' Menu
Start Date: ....../....../........... Finish Date: ....../....../...........
Notes: ....

Habit 62 - Meditate
Start Date: ....../....../........... Finish Date: ....../....../...........
Notes: ....

Habit 63 - Visualize
Start Date: ....../....../........... Finish Date: ....../....../...........
Notes: ....

Habit 64 - Celebrate Success !
Start Date: ..../......./.......... Finish Date: ..../......./..........
Notes: ....
....

Habit 65 - Flirt!
Start Date: ..../......./.......... Finish Date: ..../......./..........
Notes: ....
....

Habit 66 - Be Kind To Me
Start Date: ..../......./.......... Finish Date: ..../......./..........
Notes: ....
....

Habit 67 - Be Kind To Others
Start Date: ..../......./.......... Finish Date: ..../......./..........
Notes: ....
....

Habit 68 - Get Up And Get It Myself
Start Date: ..../......./.......... Finish Date: ..../......./..........
Notes: ....
....

Habit 69 - Be Grateful
Start Date: ..../......./.......... Finish Date: ..../......./..........
Notes: ....
....

Habit 70 - Water Down Coffee
Start Date: ..../......./.......... Finish Date: ..../......./..........
Notes: ....
....

Habit 71 - Get Organized
Start Date: ....../....../........... Finish Date: ....../....../...........
Notes: ....

Habit 72 - Eat Sandwiches With 1 Slice Of Bread
Start Date: ....../....../........... Finish Date: ....../....../...........
Notes: ....

Habit 73 - Laugh!
Start Date: ....../....../........... Finish Date: ....../....../...........
Notes: ....

Habit 74 - Hug!
Start Date: ....../....../........... Finish Date: ....../....../...........
Notes: ....

Habit 75 - Walk A Dog
Start Date: ....../....../........... Finish Date: ....../....../...........
Notes: ....

Habit 76 - Learn To Dance
Start Date: ....../....../........... Finish Date: ....../....../...........
Notes: ....

Habit 77 - Do Shower Exercises
Start Date: ....../....../........... Finish Date: ....../....../...........
Notes: ....

Habit 78 - Park An Exercise Machine In Front Of TV
Start Date: ..../......./............ Finish Date: ..../......./............
Notes: ....

Habit 79 - Teach A Child To Play Ball
Start Date: ..../......./............ Finish Date: ..../......./............
Notes: ....

Habit 80 - Take Up A Sport
Start Date: ..../......./............ Finish Date: ..../......./............
Notes: ....

Habit 81 - Do Gardening
Start Date: ..../......./............ Finish Date: ..../......./............
Notes: ....

Habit 82 - Bike To Shops
Start Date: ..../......./............ Finish Date: ..../......./............
Notes: ....

Habit 83 - Beat Out Frustrations
Start Date: ..../......./............ Finish Date: ..../......./............
Notes: ....

Habit 84 - Walk Up And Down Escalators
Start Date: ..../......./............ Finish Date: ..../......./............
Notes: ....

Habit 85 - Have More Sex
Start Date: ....../....../........... Finish Date: ....../....../...........
Notes: ....

Habit 86 - Learn To Play The Drums
Start Date: ....../....../........... Finish Date: ....../....../...........
Notes: ....

Notes

....

....

....

....

....

....

....

....

....

....

....

....

....

....

Notes

....

....

....

....

....

....

....

....

....

....

....

....

....

....

....